Among the Iceber
RMS Titanic in phot

The *Titanic* afloat on the river Lagan after the successful launch and waiting to be towed away from the slipway. The launch date also coincided with the departure of the *Olympic* to Liverpool, following the successful completion of her trials the previous day.

White Star Offices, Liverpool

First published by Brampton Publications, 1987
reprinted 1988,
reprinted 1995, 1996, 1997, 1998 by S.B. Publications
as RMS *Titanic* - a portrait in old picture postcards
this new revised edition published 2011
by Stenlake Publishing Ltd
54-58 Mill Square, Catrine, KA5 6RD
01290 551122
www.stenlake.co.uk
ISBN 9781840335378

The publishers regret that they cannot supply
copies of any pictures featured in this book.

printed by: Blissetts, Roslin Road, Acton, W3 8DH

ACKNOWLEDGEMENTS

The authors are indebted to the following, without whom this book would not have been possible: Bamforth & Co. Ltd., Holmfirth, Huddersfield for their kind permission to reproduce the set of six 'In Memoriam' postcards in their song card series. Steve Benz for his original idea, research and editing. The majority of the postcards illustrated have been selected from the authors' collections.

The offices of the White Star Line in Britain were based in Liverpool. The company was owned by and part of the giant International Mercantile Marine Company, founded by J. P. Morgan and whose president was Joseph Bruce Ismay. Fierce competition existed for the lucrative transatlantic passenger market and following Cunard's success with the *Lusitania* and *Mauretania* both launched in 1906, White Star planned in early 1907 to build two giant luxury liners (later joined by a third), providing a weekly express service from Southampton to New York. These ships were named *Olympic*, *Titanic* and *Gigantic* (the latter subsequently changed to *Britannic*).

FOREWORD (to the 1987 edition)
by Donald Smith, great nephew to Captain E. J. Smith, Master of the *Titanic*

I am delighted to have been asked to write a foreword to this new book about the *Titanic*, illustrating the story of this great ship in old picture postcards.

My earliest recollection of the existence and fame of my great uncle, Captain Edward John Smith, was a visit to Lichfield in Staffordshire to view the statue in Beacon Park, when I was seven years old. I often return to visit the statue and always gain a great sense of pride seeing the Captain there. I was very interested to discover that the statue was sculptured by Lady Kathleen Scott, wife to Captain Robert Scott, the famous British Antarctic explorer.

In 1985 I started a campaign to have the statue returned to Hanley, Stoke-on-Trent, the home town of Captain Smith. I wrote to Stoke City Council with this idea in mind and in September of the same year, they approached Lichfield District Council and formally asked for the statue to be returned. I had offered to pay for the cost of transportation. Unfortunately, this request was refused by Lichfield Council in 1986. This was naturally a great disappointment because my family would dearly love to see the statue brought back to the Potteries, where it rightfully belongs.

I am very fortunate to own some of my great uncle's possessions, which include one of his sextants, the telescope that he used when he was Master of the *Olympic*, a pocket watch and one of his cigar holders in its original case.

I wish Brampton Publications every success with this new book and may the memory of the *Titanic* live on forever.

Donald Smith,
Hanley, Stoke-on-Trent.

Captain Smith Memorial and Recreation Grounds, Lichfield.

Captain Smith's memorial, Lichfield, Staffordshire. The memorial is made of bronze and stands 7 feet 8 inches on a plinth of Cornish granite. It was sculptured by Lady Kathleen Scott (1878-1947), widow of Captain Robert Falcon Scott, C.V.O., R.N., the famous Antarctic explorer. The formal unveiling of the statue took place on 29th July 1914 by Helen Smith, daughter of Captain Smith, in the presence of Lady Scott. On the front of the plinth the memorial plate reads:

Cdr. Edward John Smith, R.D., R.N.R. Born 27th Jan. 1850. Died 15th April 1912. Bequeathing to his countrymen the memory and example of a great heart, a brave life and a heroic death. "Be British"

INTRODUCTION

The loss of the *Titanic* on Monday 15th April 1912 has remained the world's worst maritime disaster during peacetime. Public interest and debate concerning the loss of the luxury White Star passenger liner, at the time the world's largest ship, has continued over the last 75 years and in particular, following the rediscovery of her last resting place by the Woods Hole Oceanographic Team in 1985 and again in 1986.

Many excellent and authoritative books have been written about the *Titanic* and the aim of this book is to illustrate the story of the ship, but using old picture postcards, which have become some of the rarest and most valuable postcards collected today.

The authors have selected the best postcards from their collections and follow in sequence the building, launch, trials, maiden voyage and disaster of the *Titanic*. These are followed by a selection of In Memoriam postcards and some unusual postcards published after the loss of the ship.

During the Edwardian era, known to postcard collectors as the 'Golden Age of Postcards', a national craze of collecting postcards existed in this country. Postcard publishers produced vast numbers of cards depicting every subject imaginable, and naturally a national disaster was a prime subject to feature. The national craze died out with the commencement of the First World War and postcard sales dropped dramatically with the rise in postage rates and the increased use of the telephone. Many collections were forgotten but were rediscovered when the hobby started to become popular in the mid 1970s. During the last ten years it has become one of the fastest growing collecting hobbies, with new collectors joining the hobby annually.

Amongst the more sought after postcards are those depicting the *Titanic*. The rarest cards are those that were issued and postally used before the date of the disaster. After 15th April 1912 postcard publishers issued a wide variety of postcards. These more common and less valuable cards can offer a fascinating study to the story of the *Titanic*, with publishers even printing incorrect details about the ship.

The postcards illustrated in this book are not a definitive list, but offer collectors an idea to the range of postcards available. The authors would be pleased to learn of any new postcards owned by other collectors not featured in this book.

Mark Bown and Roger Simmons
July 1987.

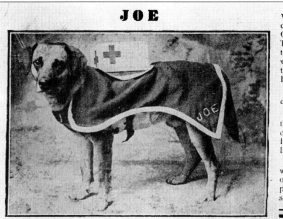

Following the disaster, there was an immediate call to organise a relief fund for the families of passengers and crew, who had been lost with the *Titanic*. The London Lord Mayor's Fund was established and with the efforts of fund-raising around the country, the fund exceeded £413,200. Among postcards which exist illustrating fund-raising activities, this delightful card shows 'Joe', who collected money for charity, including the *Titanic* disaster fund, by receiving donations placed in the box strapped to his back.

Harland and Wolff, the Belfast Shipbuilders were chosen to build the three new ships, through their close association with White Star and having built the majority of the company's ships. The chairman of Harland and Wolff, Lord Pirrie would be responsible for their design and the Rt. Hon. Alexander Carlisle would be responsible for the general construction, decoration and equipment. The order was placed for the *Olympic* and *Titanic* on 1st July 1907 and the two ships were given the shipyard numbers 400 and 401 respectively. Major alterations were made at the shipyard with two special slipways constructed, numbers 2 and 3. These were in turn surmounted by an enormous Arrol gantry, built especially for the construction of the two ships. The *Olympic's* keel was laid on 1st January 1909 and its outline can be seen in the centre of the postcard. To the right, preparations are being made for the *Titanic's* keel, which was laid on 31st March 1909.

The two ships were constructed side by side, with the *Olympic's* progress a few months ahead of the *Titanic*. Following the two keels being laid, the vertical keels and then the floors were positioned. This was followed by the framing, which was completed on the *Olympic* by 20th November 1909. Interior work on the beams, deck plating and shell plating was completed on the *Olympic* by April 1910. By this date the *Titanic* had been fully framed. The postcard illustrates the stern view of both ships at this stage of the construction.

A forward view of the two giant sister ships with the framed *Titanic* on the left, and the *Olympic* nearing completion on the right. The Arrol gantry built for the construction of the two ships consisted of three rows of towers spaced 121 feet between the rows, and each row having eleven towers, spaced 80 feet apart. The top of the towers were connected by girders fore and aft and mounted on the structure were one central revolving crane, ten walking cranes and six travelling frames, three over each berth and each carrying two cranes. Access to the structure was by four lifts and inclined walkways. The total area exceeded 840 feet long by 270 feet wide. The total height was 228 feet and the weight of the entire structure was 6000 tons.

The *Olympic* on the stocks prior to her launch, with shipyard workers visible on the deck and walkways, dwarfed by the huge size of the hull. After ten months from the keel being laid, the *Olympic* was launched on 20th October 1910 in the presence of the Lord Lieutenant of Ireland, J. Pierpoint Morgan and J. Bruce Ismay. The launch took just 62 seconds to complete. After the launch the *Olympic* was moored at the deep water wharf for the fitting of its machinery and then taken to the graving dock on 1st April 1911 for its final fitting out. It was completed by the end of May 1911, just over seven months from the launch.

The centre anchor was made to Hall's stockless patent design by Messrs. N. Hingley and Sons Ltd., of Netherton, Dudley, and weighed 16 tons 11 cwt. Due to the size of the *Titanic*, the centre anchor was made to supplement the two side bower anchors, each weighing 7 ¾ tons, and was positioned in a well immediately below the stem. A crane was fitted on the forecastle for lifting the anchor and the wire hawser, which led through an extra hawsepipe in the stem, was made to 9 ½" circumference, 175 fathoms long and supplied by Messrs. Bullivant of London. The photograph shows the anchor loaded on its carriage prior to despatch for Belfast from Hingley's works.

When the centre anchor was despatched from Hingley's works, a twenty-horse team was required to transport it to the nearest rail sidings for carriage to Harland and Wolff's yard in Belfast. All three anchors were fitted before the launch.

The cable links for the centre anchor were also made by N. Hingley & Sons Ltd. This interesting postcard shows the comparison in size of the links to some of the men who forged them. The links were 5 ¾″ and 6 ¼″ diameter and at the time were the largest links ever made.

A further comparison of the cable size with its necessary swivel arrangement, with one of the foundry workers at Hingley's works.

The *Titanic* nearing completion under the deserted gantry in the empty shipyard, suggesting that this photograph was taken on a Sunday, shortly before the launch. During the construction of the *Titanic*, the shipyard ensured the highest standards of design and used hydraulic riveting to give the best quality plating, which was completed by 19th October 1910. The total cost of the *Titanic*, including equipment was approximately £1.5 million.

Final preparations are made before the launch of the *Titanic*. The photograph clearly shows the plating arrangement to the hull, and the forward launching cradle and bracket assembly by the gantry's inclined walkway. The two hydraulic launching triggers that held the vessel when all the shores and blocks were removed, were positioned close to the launching cradle. In the left foreground can be seen the temporary platform for the dignitaries to view the launch.

The *Titanic* was launched on 31st May 1911 at 12.15 p.m. The whole procedure took 62 seconds and was witnessed by more than 100,000 people, again including J. Pierpont Morgan and J. Bruce Ismay. The quantity of lubricants used during the launch included twenty three tons of tallow, train oil and soft soap. Controlling her speed down the slip were three anchors each side and 80 tons of cable.

Five tugs were used to manoeuvre the *Titanic* after the launch, and this rare photograph shows the *Titanic* being towed to its deep water berth for the fitting out. Note also the crowded decks of the paddle steamer listing to port with the fortunate passengers having had a close-up view of the launch.

Some of the 19,000 men employed by Harland & Wolff, who built the *Olympic* and the *Titanic*, and assembled for this photograph at the fitting out basin, with the *Titanic* in the background. All the equipment, machinery, interior decorations and final construction to her superstructure would be carried out here. In comparison to the *Olympic*, slight modifications were made to her design resulting in her becoming the largest passenger vessel in the world.

WHITE STAR LINE

THE LARGEST STEAMER IN THE WORLD.

R.M.S. "OLYMPIC" TRIPLE SCREW 45,324 TONS

Statistics of the *Olympic*	Statistics of the *Titanic*
Length 882 feet. 6 inches;	Length 882 feet 9 inches;
Breadth 92 feet. 6 inches;	Breadth 92 feet. 6 inches;
Draught 34 ft. 7 ins;	Draught 34 feet. 7 inches;
Gross tonnage 45,324 tons;	Gross tonnage 46,328 tons;

Reciprocating engines provided 46,000 horse power and drove two outer propellers and one centre 'ahead only' propeller. The engines were powered by 24 double and five single-ended boilers. The design incorporated a double bottom, with sixteen watertight compartments, with the ship capable of still floating with any two of these compartments flooded. The 'unsinkable' ships were built with maximum safety and comfort for the passengers. The ships were designed and capable of moderate speeds to ensure and eliminate unnecessary vibration. Only sixteen wooden lifeboats and four collapsible canvas lifeboats were installed, giving a maximum carrying capacity of 1,167 persons. Her passenger certificate stated that she could carry a total of 3,547 persons, passengers and crew. During the building of the two ships, White Star's publicity department issued this postcard based on a painting by Montague Black, to advertise the new luxury service to New York.

The *Olympic* left Belfast on 31st May 1911 and proceeded to Southampton, via Liverpool, arriving on 2nd June 1911. She was the first ship to use the new White Star dock, which had been built to accommodate these extra large vessels. On 14th June 1911 the *Olympic* sailed on her maiden voyage to New York averaging 21.17 knots on her outward passage and 22.32 knots on her return. This is an early photograph of the *Olympic* as the ship still has a single row of lifeboats.

Both the *Olympic* and *Titanic* were fitted out to the same magnificent standard. As postcard interior views of the *Titanic* are extremely rare, six postcards of the *Olympic's* interior have been featured to illustrate the luxury that the passengers on the *Titanic* would have experienced. The first class accommodation equalling the finest hotels, extended over five decks with access between decks provided by two grand staircases, stairways and three electric lifts. The first class public rooms included the dining saloon, reception room, restaurant, lounge, reading and writing room, smoking room and a verandah cafe, known as the Cafe Parisien. The dining saloon viewed above was 114 feet long by 92 feet wide (the full width of the ship). It was decorated in Jacobean style based on observations of Haddon Hall, with the walls and ceilings painted white. Dining accommodation was provided for 532 passengers.

The first class lounge was situated on the promenade deck and decorated in the Louis Quinze style, based on observations of the Palace at Versailles. The lounge was 59 feet long, 63 feet wide and 12 feet 3 inches high. To the left of the picture and directly opposite the fireplace was a large bookcase. Behind the finely carved wall on the right was the reading and writing room.

The first class smoking room was situated towards the after-end of the promenade deck. It was designed in an early Georgian style and based on observations of houses of that period. The smoking room was 65 feet long, 63 feet wide and 12 feet 3 inches high, with the walls panelled with mahogany. The door in the right background led to the verandahs and palm courts. Additional first class features included a gymnasium, squash court, Turkish bath and a swimming pool.

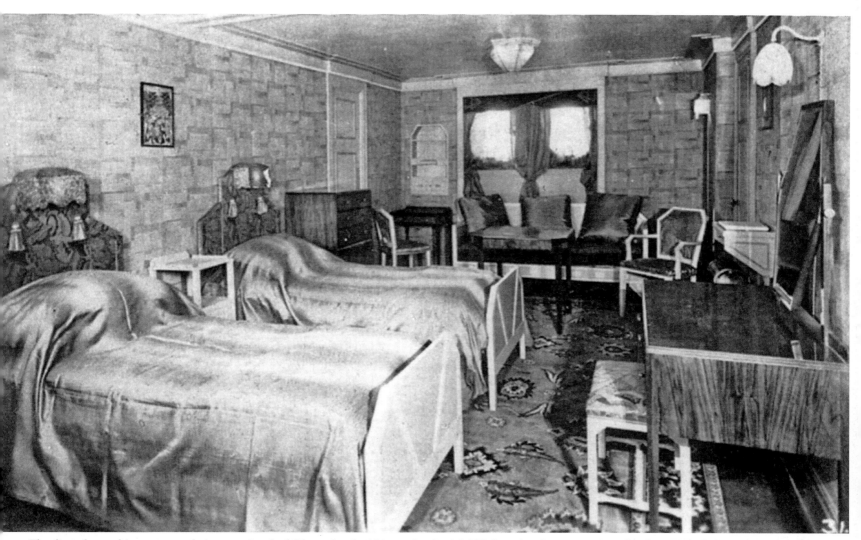

The first class cabin accommodation consisted of 96 one berth, 106 two berth and 127 three berth state rooms, plus four Parlour Suite sitting rooms, accommodating a total number of 735 first class passengers. All the state rooms were very luxurious and designed in a variety of period styles. The postcard illustration of a first class two berth cabin, was photographed at a later stage in the life of the *Olympic* but does give an idea to the size of the cabins.

The second class accommodation extended over seven decks in the after-end of the ship, with access between the decks by a grand staircase and an electric lift. The public rooms included a large dining saloon, smoking room and library. There were also 207 second class bedrooms for 674 passengers. The dining saloon viewed above was on the saloon deck, close to the kitchen. It was 71 feet long and extended the full width of the ship. Decorated in an Early English style with oak panelling it provided seating for 394 people.

The third class accommodation was of a very high standard. The public rooms included a dining saloon, seating 473 passengers, a general room and a smoking room, which were both situated on opposite sides of the poop deck. There were 222 bedrooms accommodating 862 passengers and open berths for 164 passengers. The third class lounge viewed above is a later illustration of the original third class general room. It was 36 feet long and 38 feet wide, panelled in pine and finished in white enamel. The original seating consisted of long wooden settees, tables and chairs.

During the forenoon of 20th September 1911 *Olympic* set out on her fifth voyage from Southampton under the command of Capt. E. J. Smith. As the ship rounded Calshot Spit, negotiating the difficult reverse S-turn known as the Bramble, to turn into Spithead and travelling at moderate speed, a cruiser H.M.S. *Hawke* was sighted coming up the Solent three miles away. The alteration of the *Olympic's* course to turn into Spithead caused the two ships to become parallel with each other and at a distance of 100 – 300 yards apart. Suddenly the *Hawke* altered to port to pass astern of the liner and during this action a collision occurred, with the *Hawke* hitting the *Olympic* 80 feet from the stern, on the starboard quarter. The *Hawke's* bows were badly damaged, with the collision causing a 40 feet long gash on the *Olympic*. The *Olympic's* passengers were disembarked at Cowes and the photograph below shows the ship returning to Southampton for inspection.

At the collision inquiry, the Admiralty gave evidence that the liner had crowded the channel, the *Hawke's* helm had jammed and the cruiser had been drawn in towards the liner, through the suction caused by the difference in displacements of the two vessels. The inquiry found the *Olympic* to blame, with no blame attached to the White Star Line, because the liner was being piloted. An appeal was made, but both The Court of Appeal and the House of Lords upheld the ruling.

S CRIBB
1.

THE SOLENT COLLISION.
THE OLYMPIC, AT S'AMPTON.
SHOWING THE HOLE IN THE
STARBOARD QUARTER.

A further view of the gaping hole and buckled plates with officials and workers inspecting the damage in Southampton Dock. The postcard was posted on 29th September 1911 with the message "Saw this boat in docks, she has an enormous hole in the back". The *Olympic* returned to Belfast under reduced speed for immediate repairs. She was dry docked on 6th October for six weeks with shipyard workers being transferred from the *Titanic* to quickly complete the repairs.

On 24th February 1912 the *Olympic* lost a propeller blade while crossing the Atlantic on her way to Southampton, and was once again returned to Belfast for repairs. The *Titanic* meanwhile was nearing her final completion and had to vacate the Thompson graving dock, as it was the only dry dock big enough to fit the liner for its repairs. The postcard shows the *Olympic* (left) being edged into the dry dock for her propeller blade to be replaced on 6th March 1912.

One month before completion, the *Titanic* had an additional feature made that was to distinguish her from the *Olympic*. The forward half of the promenade deck was plated and enclosed with windows, to protect the passengers from sea spray. Ten months after the launch, the *Titanic* was finally completed. Sea trials were scheduled for 1st April 1912, but due to strong north-west winds, the trials were postponed. At 6 a.m. on 2nd April 1912, five tugs were attached to the *Titanic* and guided her down Victoria Channel to Belfast Lough. The photograph shows the *Titanic* shortly before the tugs cast off and commencing her trials under her own power. The trials included manoeuvring the vessel at different speeds, testing the effectiveness of her helm and conducting an emergency stop, which took the ship just less than half a mile to come to rest after travelling at 20 knots. The *Titanic* returned to Belfast Lough by 7 p.m. She received her passenger certificate after the successful completion of the trials and disembarked the observers from Harland and Wolff.

Under the command of Captain E. J. Smith, who had earlier transferred from the *Olympic*, the *Titanic* left Belfast at 8 p.m. on the same day of her trials and commenced the voyage down the Irish Sea and St. George's Channel, around Land's End into the English Channel and up to Southampton. The postcard shows a further view of the *Titanic* being guided and towed into Belfast Lough before her trials, by the tugs *Huskisson* and *Herculaneum* at her stern and *Hornby* on her starboard bow. The tugs *Hercules* and *Herald* are hidden from view.

S.S. TITANIC.

Right: The *Titanic* arrived at Southampton late in the evening of 3rd April, and just after midnight docked at Berth 44. On Thursday 4th April, preparations began to load the ship and prepare it for its maiden voyage. The following day was Good Friday and the photograph shows the *Titanic* at her best, dressed overall in flags for the benefit of the people of Southampton. Many came to view her from the harbour or from an excursion steamer. None of the general public were allowed on board.

S.S. TITANIC AT SOUTHAMPTON.

There had been a coal strike in the country since January 1912 which was finally settled on 6th April 1912. The shortage of coal resulted in the *Titanic* being fuelled by coal taken from five other company owned ships that were docked at Southampton. The coal strike had also caused widespread unemployment in Southampton and on Saturday 6th April the majority of the crew were recruited.

Bottled beer stocks prior to loading. The *Titanic* also loaded the following supplies and catering equipment:

Fresh Meat 75,000 lbs.	Flour 250 barrels	Sugar 5 tons	Electroplate 26,000 pieces
Poultry 25,000 lbs.	Tea 1,000 lbs.	Potatoes 40 tons	Crockery 57,600 pieces
Fresh Eggs 35,000	Fresh Milk 1,500 gallons	Minerals 12,000 bottles	Glass 29,000 pieces
Cereals 10,000 lbs.	Fresh Cream 300 gallons.	Wines 1,000 bottles	Cutlery 44,000 pieces

A wide variety of general cargo of all descriptions and weighing 559 tons was also loaded.

Captain Smith and deck officers of the *Titanic* photographed on board the ship prior to the maiden voyage from Southampton.
Back row left to right:
Herbert W. McElroy, Chief Purser; Charles H. Lightoller, Second Officer, (Survived); Herbert J. Pitman, Third Officer, (Survived);
Joseph G. Boxall, Fourth Officer, (Survived), Harold G. Lowe, Fifth Officer, (Survived).
Front row left to right:
James P. Moody, Sixth Officer; Henry T. Wilde, Chief Officer; Captain Edward John Smith, R.D., R.N.R.;
William M. Murdoch, First Officer, (who was on the bridge at the time the *Titanic* struck the iceberg).

Right: Edward (Teddy) John Smith was born on 27th January 1850 in Hanley, Stoke-on-Trent, Staffordshire. He was educated at Hanley and Etruria British Schools. After leaving school he joined the Merchant Navy and joined the White Star Line in 1880, taking his first command of the steamship *Republic* in 1887. His other earlier commands included *Britannic, Germanic, Majestic* and the *Baltic*, his tenth command. Captain Smith was White Star's senior captain and also the highest paid, serving on the North Atlantic service. He was appointed Master of the *Olympic* for its maiden voyage in June 1911 and transferred to the *Titanic* to join the ship in Belfast for its trials and preparations for the maiden voyage at the beginning of April 1912. He was shortly due to retire and his appointment to the *Titanic* was considered the height of his career.

Above: An unusual photograph, showing the third and fourth funnels and the centre section of the *Titanic*. The fourth or 'dummy' funnel was used for ventilation purposes only and it is interesting to note how many pictures of the *Titanic* show the liner with smoke issuing from all four funnels. On the reverse of the photograph, a note reads: "*Titanic* with Fred's yacht alongside just prior to departure from Southampton".

S.S. TITANIC leaving Southampton on her Maiden Voyage April 10, 1912

By early Wednesday morning, 10th April 1912, all the crew had been mustered on board and were making final preparations, checking equipment and passengers lists. The complement of officers and crew totalled 898 men and women. Later the same morning, the boat trains arrived at the dockside with 180 first class, 240 second class and 494 third class passengers joining the *Titanic* for its maiden voyage. At just after 12 noon, the *Titanic* cast off from Berth 44, piloted by George Bowyer and assisted by six tugs. Among the 914 passengers on board were many famous people. These included Mr. Bruce Ismay, Chairman of White Star and Mr. Thomas Andrews, Managing Director of Harland and Wolff, with eight representatives from the shipyard. There were no fewer than ten millionaires, whose combined capital totalled £120 million, including Colonel J. J. Astor and his wife members of one of the wealthiest families in the world. In the company of this elite group were, the Countess of Rothes, many industrialists, and bankers.

As the *Titanic* proceeded down the River Test, she approached the two liners *Oceanic* and *New York* moored in tandem at Berth 38. The turbulence caused by the propellers and the variation of water displacement from the passing *Titanic* resulted in a tremendous strain on the ropes securing both ships. The ropes on the *Oceanic* held, but those holding the *New York* snapped and the liner broke away from her moorings and started to swing sternwards in an arc towards the *Titanic*. The *Titanic* was put astern and the resultant flow of water was sufficient to halt the *New York* within twelve feet of her stern. The *New York* was secured to a tug and towed and moored downstream. This incident delayed her departure for an hour and when all was clear, the *Titanic* once again proceeded towards Southampton Water.

A rare postcard postally used on 7th May 1912 illustrating the *Titanic* underway in Southampton Water. The postcard has an interesting message on its reverse: "This is the photo I promised you, taken as she is going around the corner at Ryde heading straight away for Cherbourg. You will see the only difference between her and the *Olympic* is her top deck, covered in back to her third funnel. She is three inches longer and a trifle wider to make the extra 1000 tons (46,000) against the *Olympic's* (45,000)".

Above: A distant photograph of the *Titanic* passing between two destroyers at the naval anchorage in Spithead. Laurence Beesley, a second class passenger and a teacher from Dulwich College, London noted that the ship had earlier exchanged salutes with one of the White Star tugs waiting for one of the White Star liners homeward bound. Close to the Nab lightship, the *Titanic* reduced her speed, which allowed the waiting pilot cutter to collect the pilot, George Bowyer. The liner then made her way across the English Channel to Cherbourg.

The *Titanic* arrived at Cherbourg and anchored close to the harbour at 6.30 p.m. on 10th April. Two White Star tenders, *Nomadic* and *Traffic* ferried 274 passengers (142 first class, 30 second class and 102 third class) and additional bags of mail out to the waiting liner. Many of the first class 'society' passengers had just finished the 'Season' in Europe, and among them was the millionaire, Mr. B. Guggenheim. At 8 p.m. the tenders returned to harbour and the *Titanic* weighed anchor and set course for Queenstown in Southern Ireland. The White Star water-colour postcard (right) would have been freely available on board and many would have been mailed by passengers from Cherbourg or Queenstown.

The passage to Queenstown took twenty hours and the *Titanic* anchored two miles offshore at 11.30 a.m. on Thursday 11th April. 120 passengers (seven second class and 113 third class) and further bags of mail were ferried out by the tenders, *America* and *Ireland*. Many of the passengers were emigrants to America. At 1.30 p.m. the liner weighed anchor and departed from Queenstown for New York. The total passenger complement of 1,308 now included 322 first class, 277 second class and 709 third class passengers. The artist drawn postcard of the *Olympic* above, complete with the Statue of Liberty conspicuous on the left, was titled *Titanic*.

Throughout Sunday 14th April the radio room, manned by Jack Phillips and his assistant Harold Bride, had received and reported many warnings about the existence of an extensive field of pack ice and icebergs that had drifted south into the main shipping lanes. By the evening, the air temperature had fallen to 31°F and the ship's carpenter was instructed to watch that the fresh water tanks did not freeze. The night was clear and with good visibility the ship maintained a speed of 22 knots. Just after 11.30 p.m. the lookout in the crow's nest sounded a warning of three bells and phoned the bridge with the message, "Iceberg, right ahead".

SS TITANIC IN MID-ATLANTIC
PASSING ICE BERGS
FOUNDERED ON HER
MAIDEN VOYAGE
APRIL 15 1912

First Officer Murdoch on duty on the bridge immediately ordered "Full Astern", "Hard-a-starboard" and closed the watertight doors. This prompt action prevented a direct collision, but the iceberg struck the *Titanic* below the waterline on its starboard side, buckling the plates and opening the seams. Water flooded in along a 300 foot gash extending from number one hold to number six boiler room. Captain Smith appeared on the bridge and with Thomas Andrews calculated that the ship would not last much longer than two hours. Fourth Officer Boxall meanwhile calculated that the ship's position was 41° 46′ N, 50° 14′ W. At 12.05 a.m.. Captain Smith gave the order to uncover the boats and assemble crew and passengers.

TITANIC DISASTER APRIL 15TH 1912
1,635 PERISH AT SEA
(1) CAPTAIN SMITH (2) PHILLIPS, THE HERO OPERATOR.
3. RESCUING A PASSENGER. Bonner Arcade House
Whitley Bay.

S.S. Titanic, foundered April 16th 1912.
"Their promised land fades from view."

Captain Smith took the calculated ship's position to the radio operator, Jack Phillips, who transmitted the distress signal, C.Q.D. at 12.15 a.m.. At 12.25 a.m. the Cunard-owned *Carpathia* which was 58 miles away to the south-east, answered the distress call and immediately altered course to the north-west, speeding at seventeen knots to assist the *Titanic*. At the same time, the order was given to load the lifeboats. At 12.45 a.m. the first boat (number 7) was lowered, with less than half its capacity on board. Eight distress rockets were fired at five minute intervals from the bridge, who also noticed about six miles away the navigation lights of a mysterious vessel that appeared, turned and then vanished. Jack Phillips commenced using the new distress signal S.O.S. (the first time it was used by a passenger liner). Eleven ships heard *Titanic's* signals but the majority were too far away to render assistance quickly. Following the order that women and children were to have priority, there were many separations of husbands and wives. Many husbands had to force their wives into the boats, while some wives refused to leave their husbands. Many lifeboats were lowered without their full capacity and by 1.25 a.m., the remaining lifeboats were being overloaded. At 1.30 a.m., panic started by boat 14, resulting in Fifth Officer Lowe firing a revolver to control the passengers. By now the liner had settled well into the water and the last of the rigid lifeboats (number 4) was launched at 1.55 a.m. Of the four remaining collapsible canvas lifeboats, 'C' and 'D' were launched successfully, with Bruce Ismay managing to escape in 'C' boat. Boats 'A' and 'B' became impossible to launch, but during the last moments were dislodged and managed to float away from the ship, upside down. At 2.05 a.m., Capt. Smith dismissed the two radio operators from their duties, but Phillips stayed on for a further fifteen minutes while there was enough power on board. At 2.10 a.m., the bow became deeply submerged and the stern lifted above the water. As the angle rose towards the vertical, the forward funnel snapped from its mountings and a terrible roar was heard as all the moveable objects broke free and crashed downwards. By 2.20 a.m. the *Titanic* had disappeared, plunging two miles down to the ocean floor.

There were many reports about what exactly happened to Captain Smith during the last moments of the ship. One report gave details that he had shot himself on the bridge, another report said that he had saved a child, as shown on the postcard, but there is little doubt that the true report of his death was that he died on the bridge alone, after doing his duty and having given his last order to the remaining passengers and crew, "Be British". The postcard also shows an artist's impression of the collapsible lifeboat 'A' being rescued by the lifeboat commanded by Fifth Officer Lowe.

The *Carpathia* commanded by Captain Rostron, arrived at the scene of the disaster just after 3.30 a.m.. By 8.30 a.m., after a thorough search, all the survivors had been taken safely on board, and the ship proceeded to New York. Of the total of 2,206 passengers and crew, there were 703 survivors (493 passengers and 210 crew). At the same time, the *Californian* commanded by Captain Lord and owned by the Leyland Line, arrived to assist the *Carpathia* in searching for survivors. Later there was to be considerable controversy that the *Californian* had been the mysterious ship sighted by the *Titanic*. Captain Lord always maintained that his ship had been stationary, surrounded by ice and having seen white rockets fired from a ship had tried unsuccessfully to contact it by Morse lamp. The radio operator on the *Californian* had been asleep all night, and had been unaware of the *Titanic's* signals. The *Carpathia* finally arrived with the survivors in New York on Wednesday 18th April.

When news reports were first received, the exact details of the disaster were confused, but by the evening of Tuesday 16th April, the devastating news had been confirmed. The first survivor lists were posted up on Wednesday 17th April. This photograph of J. C. Clark's corner grocers shop, somewhere in north-west England, was taken shortly after the sinking of the *Titanic*. On the right of the picture the newspaper boards announce headlines from the Daily Sketch, -TITANIC'S FAREWELL' and the Daily News, -TITANIC DISASTER - LIST OF THE SURVIVORS'.

SOLDIERS COLLECTING TITANIC MEMORIAL
APRIL 28TH 1912 PHOTO R45

The city of Southampton suffered terribly following the news of disaster, with many families being afflicted by the loss of their loved ones, especially the members of the crew who had drowned. The city set up its own disaster fund and this postcard, postally used 6th May 1912 and taken from a series, illustrates soldiers collecting for the fund. The date of 28th April suggests that this was photographed at the open-air service held at the Marlands, Southampton to celebrate the return of surviving members of the crew. It was attended by over 50,000 people.

NURSES COLLECTING FOR TITANIC FUND
APRIL 28TH 1912 PHOTO No8

Another postcard in the same series and illustrating nurses collecting for the *Titanic* fund, set up by the city of Southampton. The proceeds of the fund would have helped to relieve financial hardship for the widows and children of lost crewmen. Some of the surviving members of the crew arrived in Southampton, after travelling from Plymouth by train, late in the evening of Sunday 28th April, 1912. Other members arrived later, to be reunited with their families on Tuesday 30th April.

Within three days of the disaster publishers were producing 'In Memoriam' postcards because of the tremendous public interest in the loss of the ship. Numerous varieties were published with some containing factual errors. The postcard illustrated above is one of the best examples of an 'In Memoriam' card (other examples are illustrated opposite) and was published by E. A. Bragg of Falmouth. The photograph of the *Titanic* was taken when departing from Southampton. John Phillips was the senior radio operator and sent the first C.Q.D. (Come Quickly, Distress) signal at 12.15 a.m. on 15th April 1912.

DISASTER TO THE "TITANIC": WORLD'S LARGEST SHIP
COLLIDES WITH AN ICEBERG IN THE ATLANTIC
DURING HER MAIDEN VOYAGE APRIL 15 - 1912.

PHOTOS SHOW - THE TITANIC IN THE SOLENT APRIL 10
MR W T STEAD THE FAMOUS JOURNALIST DROWNED

A BRITISH WARSHIP PASSING. AN ATLANTIC ICEBERG

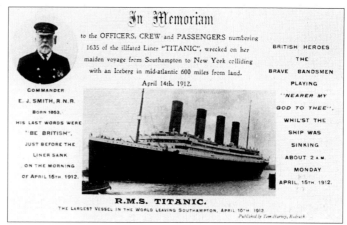

In Memoriam

to the OFFICERS, CREW and PASSENGERS numbering
1635 of the ill-fated Liner "TITANIC", wrecked on her
maiden voyage from Southampton to New York colliding
with an Iceberg in mid-atlantic 600 miles from land.

April 14th. 1912.

COMMANDER
E. J. SMITH, R.N.R.
BORN 1853.
HIS LAST WORDS WERE
"BE BRITISH".
JUST BEFORE THE
LINER SANK
ON THE MORNING
OF APRIL 15TH 1912.

BRITISH HEROES
THE
BRAVE BANDSMEN
PLAYING
"NEARER MY
GOD TO THEE",
WHIL'ST THE
SHIP WAS
SINKING
ABOUT 2 A.M.
MONDAY
APRIL 15TH 1912.

R.M.S. TITANIC.
THE LARGEST VESSEL IN THE WORLD LEAVING SOUTHAMPTON, APRIL 10TH 1912.
Published by Tom Haney, Redruth

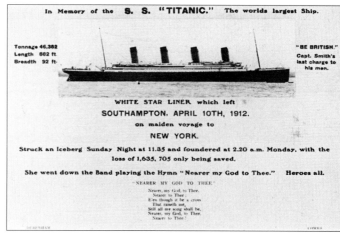

In Memory of the S. S. "TITANIC." The worlds largest Ship.

Tonnage 46,382
Length 882 ft.
Breadth 92 ft.

"BE BRITISH."
Capt. Smith's
last charge to
his men.

WHITE STAR LINER which left
SOUTHAMPTON, APRIL 10TH, 1912.
on maiden voyage to
NEW YORK.

Struck an Iceberg Sunday Night at 11.35 and foundered at 2.20 a.m. Monday, with the
loss of 1,635, 705 only being saved.

She went down the Band playing the Hymn "Nearer my God to Thee." Heroes all.

"NEARER MY GOD TO THEE."
Nearer, my God, to Thee,
Nearer to Thee ;
E'en though it be a cross
That raiseth me,
Still all my song shall be,
Nearer, my God, to Thee,
Nearer to Thee !

Left: An unusual multi-view photographic postcard issued after the disaster its top photograph shows a British warship passing an Atlantic iceberg; the lower photograph shows the *Titanic* in the Solent on 10th April and the small inset photograph is of the famous British journalist and editor of the Pall Mall Gazette, William Thomas Stead, who was drowned during the disaster. W. T. Stead was on his way to address a peace conference at Carnegie Hall, New York that was to be held on 21st April, 1912.

Postcards illustrating the members of the ship's orchestra, who all died during the disaster. One of the great deeds of heroism that captured the public's imagination was achieved by the members of the *Titanic's* orchestra led by their bandmaster, Wallace Hartley. The orchestra continued to play popular tunes, including ragtime, right to the very end. The hymn "Nearer, my God, to Thee!" has been a legend ever since the disaster, as it was believed to have been the last piece of music played by the orchestra before the *Titanic* took its final dive. Some survivors also reported that they heard the recessional hymn tune 'Autumn' played during the last moments of the ship.

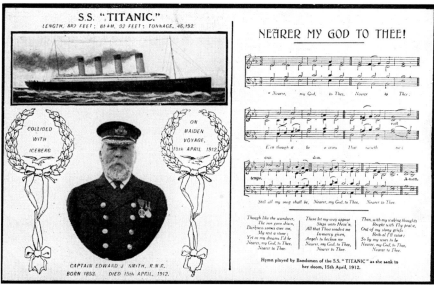

Upper left: A well-designed 'In Memoriam' postcard published by Millar and Lang in their "National" series. Details are given about the hymn, the collision and Captain Smith.

Lower left: A French postcard issued after the disaster with the words of the hymn printed in both French and English.

Above: Published by Rotary Photographic Company and illustrating the famous hymn. The postcard uses the same photograph of the *Titanic* departing Southampton as the cover of this book. The ship has been superimposed on to a different sea and the artist has drawn a new horizon and added wisps of smoke from all four funnels!

Bamforth & Company Ltd., of Holmfirth, near Huddersfield, produced a famous set of six memorial postcards for the *Titanic* illustrating the ship sinking and reproducing verses of the hymn "Nearer, My God, to Thee!", written by Arthur Sullivan. The postcards were published in two varieties: sepia and black and white.

THE ILL-FATED WHITE STAR LINER "TITANIC"
Struck an iceberg off the coast of Newfoundland on her maiden voyage, & sunk with over One Thousand Six Hundred of her Passengers & Crew, Monday morning April 15th 1912.

Numerous postcards were published following the disaster, and some publishers substituted photographs of the *Titanic's* sister ship, the *Olympic*. This could have been the result of publishers having insufficient stocks of *Titanic* postcards and not being able to satisfy the demands of the public. The photograph on the left clearly shows the *Olympic*, the main difference between the two ships being the open area on the *Olympic's* forward passenger deck, and the *Titanic* having an enclosed front forward section on the same deck below the first two funnels.

The two paintings below are further examples of images of the *Olympic* being named as the *Titanic*.

WHITE STAR LINE

T.S.S. TITANIC.

White Star Liner, "TITANIC"
Left Southampton on maiden voyage, April 10th, 1912.
Collided with icefield and sank, Monday, 15th April.
Length, 882 feet; beam, 92 feet; tonnage, 46,192.
Captain, E. J. Smith.

WHITE STAR TRIPLE-SCREW STEAMER "TITANIC" (45,000 TONS).
THE LARGEST VESSEL IN THE WORLD
FIRST VOYAGE FROM SOUTHAMPTON TO NEW YORK, WEDNESDAY, APRIL 10th, 1912.

THIS VESSEL IS LUBRICATED WITH "VACUUM" TURBINE OIL.

VACUUM OIL CO LTD
LONDON

These advertising cards were originally given away free and now are very collectable. This card issued by The Vacuum Oil Company stating that the *Titanic* is the largest vessel in the world, is actually illustrated by the *Olympic*. An artist has painted in the sea on the photograph, which must have been taken in port, as the ship has been dressed with flags. Among the other interesting features are the details of the first voyage between Southampton and New York, which are not often seen on postcards. The manager of the 'Vacuum' oil company, Howard Cane, travelled on the *Titanic* and died during the disaster.

R.M.S. TITANIC

EMPIRE PALACE
RIPLEY.
WEEK COMMENCING OCT. 5th 1914.

POST CARD.

COPYRIGHT   PRINTED & PUBLISHED BY J. SALMON, SEVENOAKS, ENGLAND   FROM AN ORIGINAL WATER COLOUR DRAWING

CHARLES W. & JOHN R. POOLE'S
GIGANTIC REPRODUCTION ILLUSTRATIVE
OF THE

LOSS of the "TITANIC"

The Immortal Tale of Simple Heroism

In Eight Tableaux, comprising :—

1. A splendid marine effect of the Gigantic Vessel gliding from the Quayside at Southampton.
2. Cork Harbour, showing the return of the White Star Tender to Queenstown and the "Titanic" outward bound.
3. MID-OCEAN. The "Titanic," brilliantly illuminated, speeding along at 21 knots.
4. The S.S. "Touraine" in the icefield, and carefully steering her way through the towering bergs.
5. The approach of the iceberg. The collision and grinding crash. Lowering out the lifeboats.
6. FOUNDERING. The great vessel sinking by the head. The extinction of the lights. The Sinking.
7. The arrival of the "Carpathia" and rescue of the survivors.
8. The Vision.

The spectacle staged in its entirety by John R Poole, and every endeavour made to convey a true pictorial idea of the whole history of the disaster

Unique Mechanical and Electric Effects, special music and the story described in a thrilling manner

THE ADDRESS ONLY TO BE WRITTEN HERE

STAMP

An advertising postcard based on a watercolour painting of the *Olympic*, announcing the showing of Charles W. and John R. Poole's gigantic reproduction illustrative show, the *Loss of the "Titanic"*, at the Empire Palace, Ripley, Derbyshire for the week commencing 5th October 1914. The same card is known to exist overprinted with different theatres in other parts of the country. The reverse side to the postcard gives details of C. W. & J. R. Poole's unique and thrilling show, utilising mechanical and electrical effects and special music.

This 'In Memoriam' postcard was published to commemorate the loss of the *Lusitania*, torpedoed by a German submarine, the *U-139* (below), off the south coast of Ireland on 7th May 1915. Amazingly, the ship illustrated is the *Titanic*, photographed when it was departing from Southampton Water on 10th April 1912. The enclosed forward section on the passenger deck gives evidence to this fact, and the tug *Vulcan* is just visible by the ship's side. The *Mauritania* (the *Lusitania's* sister ship) is pictured below for comparison.

S. BURGESS, S.S. "LUSITANIA." LONDON, W.C.

TORPEDOED BY A GERMAN SUBMARINE MAY 7, 1915.

The U-139 Which Sank the Lusitania

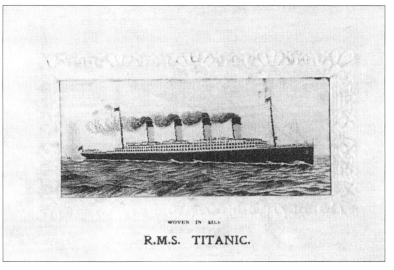

WOVEN IN SILK

R.M.S. TITANIC.

A very collectable woven silk coloured postcard produced by the firm of Thomas Stevens of Coventry. Similar postcards were also produced by W. H. Grant, also of Coventry. Woven silks were machine made and had a smooth uniform finish. Only limited numbers of these postcards were produced and this has contributed to their rarity and value today.

Le "TITANIC" jaugeant 45.000 tonnes, longueur 288 m. 977, largeur 28 m. 193, profondeur 29 m. 66, a coûté 46 millions. Coulé à 3.200 mètres de fond dans la traversée de Southampton à New-York à la suite d'un abordage avec un bloc de glace. 1.800 victimes — 16 Avril 1912

An example of a very amateurish French postcard, poorly drawn and giving incorrect details of the disaster. The early reports of the disaster were sketchy and some postcards that were published shortly after the disaster printed the wrong information. On this postcard, the details list 1,800 victims and the date of the disaster as 16th April, 1912.

Graz   „Titanic" im Hilmteich (Sicherer Hafen)

A crudely drawn sinking *Titanic* superimposed on a photograph of the boating lake in Graz, Austria. This very rare and cynical Austrian postcard, postally used on 12th June 1912, was possibly a political cartoon commenting on the qualities of British Shipbuilding.

Two Courts of Inquiry were held to investigate the loss of the *Titanic*. The American Inquiry, chaired by Senator William Smith, was held in New York between 19th April and 25th May 1912 and the British Inquiry chaired by Lord Mersey was held in London between 2nd May and 30th July 1912. The main conclusions at both Courts of Inquiry were: The speed of the *Titanic* had been too fast, taking into account the reported existence of extensive ice in the area. The ship had insufficient lifeboats for passengers and crew, some being difficult to launch and others being launched without their full complement on board. Captain Lord of the *Californian* was also criticised for not investigating the distress rockets seen by his ship. As a result of the findings of the British Inquiry, the Board of Trade introduced new safety measures, which have become universal. These measures included sufficient lifeboats on every ship for all passengers and crew, regular boat drills and a 24 hour radio watch to be maintained. The illustration shows the *Olympic* after her major refit undergone in 1912-13, costing £250,000, and showing her additional lifeboats.

The memorial to all the brave engineers, who perished on the *Titanic*, is sited in East Park, Southampton. For the unveiling ceremony, the memorial was covered by a large Union Jack, which was formally unveiled by Sir Archibald Denny on 22nd April 1914, just over two years after the disaster. It was estimated that over 100,000 people were present for the ceremony.

This memorial was erected to the memory of the firemen, sailors and stewards of the *Titanic*, and was originally located on The Common in Southampton. A special fund had been organised by the people of Southampton and the memorial was officially unveiled by Mr. Bullions Moody, treasurer to the fund, on 27th July 1915. The memorial was sculptured from Portland stone and also served as a drinking fountain. The centre urn is now missing and following vandalism to the memorial, it was removed for its protection to the ruins of Holy Rood Church in 1972. The church was badly destroyed during the Second World War and has been kept as a memorial to the Merchant Navy. The *Titanic* memorial was restored and cleaned in 1982.

Two In Memorium postcards of Wallace Hartley, the one below showing his grave. The body of the *Titanic's* bandmaster was returned to England on 12th May, 1912, on board the White Star liner *Arabic*. He was buried with full honours in his home town of Colne, Lancashire on 18th May 1912. A fine monument also exists in the town park in Colne.

The last and largest of the three sister ships was the *Britannic*. Her keel was laid on the 30th November 1911 and she was launched on 26th February 1914. As a result of the enquiries into the *Titanic's* sinking several changes were made to the design of the ship. Inevitably, the design of the watertight bulkheads within the ship was changed, in *Titanic* they reached 'E' deck; in *Britannic* six of the fifteen bulkheads extended to 'B' deck. The design of her hull was also altered to create a double hull along the engine and boiler rooms. *Britannic*, of course, also had lifeboat provision for all her passengers. To accomodate the changes the ship was wider by two feet, and had a tonnage of 48,153 tons. To compensate for her extra width and tonnage her engines were more powerful. The start of the First World War in August 1914 meant that the fitting of the ship was slowed down, since Admiralty work was given precedence. In 1915 the need for increased tonnage became apparent and *Britannic* was finished and prepared for possible service. On 13th November 1915 *Britannic* was requisitioned as a hospital ship and taken from her storage mooring in Belfast. She was repainted white, received a green stripe along her length, red crosses on her sides, and renamed H.M.H.S. (His Majesty's Hospital Ship) *Britannic*. After five sailings to and from the Mediterranean returning the sick and wounded from Gallipoli to the UK, *Britannic* made her final voyage from Southampton on 12th November 1916. At 8.12 a.m. on 21st November in the Kea Channel, off Greece, the ship hit a mine. As a result of the damage caused by the explosion the ship began to sink. By 9.07 a.m. the ship had sunk. Thirty people lost their lives in the disaster, 1,036 were saved.